IPAD GUIDE FOR THI

A STEP-BY-STEP MANUAL FOR THE NON-TECH-SAVVY TO

MASTER YOUR IPAD IN NO TIME

John Halbert

1

Sommario

Introduction

Learning a new technology is often challenging and overwhelming for seniors. But with a comprehensive guide like this, you can become a pro with your iPad device. Remember to follow the instructions and carefully practice them to understand different operations better.

Due to the adaptability and portability it offers for customers, the introduction of the iPad represents a turning point in modern technology. Steve Jobs was always captivated by computers, and he was always irritated by tablets' inferior performance compared to PCs.

This book is a resource to aid seniors in comprehending the fundamental capabilities of an iPad through clear explanations. Technology can occasionally be challenging for people for a variety of reasons. But with the right guide, you can face your concerns and benefit from technology. The iPad is a type of technology that requires some getting used to, but once you do, there are many things you can do with it.

The iPad operating systems, which Apple just introduced, are reportedly vast upgrades over the prior versions. For instance, widgets are now located on the Home screen in iPad rather than only the sidebar. In addition, the iPad offers new Contacts and Find My widgets. The App Library will be featured in iPad much like in other versions, making it accessible via the device's Dock. You may now totally conceal Home screens in this edition, along with removing any apps you might not use frequently. The Home Screen and App Library now have new widget layouts that make it simple to categorize apps and personalize the iPad experience.

The iPad has been a commercial success since it was first introduced as a digital product. Apple sold more than three million iPads in the first 90 days they were on sale. People would wait in line for hours in front of Apple stores to purchase the newest technological advancement, which would go on to become one of the most well-known portable tablets in history.

This book has ensured that the older citizens for whom it is designed may comprehend the flow and core of the subjects covered. The reader is given step-by-step instructions and sample scenarios as needed.

To get the most out of this book, all you need is an iPad model of your choice and a strong commitment to learning. Additionally, since operating the device occasionally requires Apple ID authentication, we advise having both an email address and a mobile number. Let us dive into the comprehensive iPad guide now!

Chapter 1: A brief history of the ipad since 2010

Apple released numerous iPad versions over a ten-year period to targeted consumers in various demographics. A decade ago, Apple offered a single device model for all demographics, but by 2022, it had numerous tiers of models accessible for customers with various demographics and use cases.

iPad by Apple (2010): The original iPad, which was released in January 2010, featured a 9.7-inch display and an aluminum body. Customers also had a choice between a 32GB or 64GB model in addition to the A4 CPU.

iPad 2 by Apple (2011): In 2011, the A5-powered second-generation iPad was announced. It was quite an improvement over the first-generation iPad in every way.

The front and back cameras made the iPad 2 a superb FaceTime compatible video calling device.

iPads 3 and 4 (2012): The third-generation iPad, which was introduced in 2012, had an A5X CPU and a retina display, which offered four times as many pixels than the iPads from earlier generations. With iOS6, which was included with the iPad 3, the more than 200,000 apps accessible in the App Store became more stable.

Within a short period of time, Apple's iPad 4 with its significantly speedier A6X CPU was on sale. Dual-band Wi-Fi was now supported on the iPad4 for quicker and more instantaneous internet access.

Apple Mini iPad (2012): In 2012, Apple introduced the iPad Mini series alongside the iPad 4 for the first time. The iPad mini was considerably smaller than the standard iPad models while still providing the same operating system and user-friendliness. The Mini version, on the other hand, had a 1024x768 HD display rather than a Retina display.

Apple Air iPad (2013): The fifth-generation iPad model, the iPad Air, had a new A7 CPU and 20% faster system processing. iPads now had the potential to handle greater video frame rates, making them a better choice for pros. This model's bezels were also reduced by Apple, improving it as an entertainment device.

iPad Mini 2 by Apple (2013): Apple concentrated on enhancing the display resolution and added a significantly quicker A7 chip to the iPad mini in its 2013 update. Despite having a similar design to Android tablets of the same size, it performed two times better.

iPad Air 2 by Apple (2014): The best-looking tablets were the second-generation iPad models, which boasted the slimmest designs and the A8X processor boost from Apple. The addition of Touch ID in the second-generation Air model marked a substantial departure from the first two Air models.

Apple Mini 3 and 4 (2014-2015): The iPad Mini 3 and iPad Mini 4 both received slight updates, faster A8 processors, and completely laminated displays. The resolutions of the front and back cameras were also improved. Apple, however, made the temporary decision to stop producing Mini variants after the iPad mini 4.

iPad 12.9 and 9.7 from Apple (2015): The iPad range from Apple revolutionized the potential of tablets and ensured that they were as effective as desktops and laptops. The 12.9 and 9.7 inch first-generation Pros were made available in two different sizes. With a metal build, they were also thinner and lighter. The Apple ecosystem also welcomed the Apple Pencil, a brand-new stylus, along with the iPad Pro tablets. The iPad's stunning Retina display, which had more pixels and a lightning-fast refresh rate, was the key benefit. Even today the best tablets for professionals are iPad Pros.

iPad by Apple (2017–2021): Despite the popularity of the Apple iPad Pro, Apple didn't completely disregard the low-end iPad models, which also do well and appeal to a wide range of consumers, including regular users and students. The entry-level Apple iPad is the least expensive tablet that Apple has recently provided to customers.

The older Apple silicon processor used in all of the entry-level iPad models performs more than three times better than that found in Android tablets. Additionally, the same operating system, iPad OS, runs on virtually every variation of the iPad. Apple Keyboard and Apple Pencil are also compatible with the standard iPad.

Apple iPad Pro models released in 2017–2020: The best tablets right now are all of the more recent iPad models. For the Pro models, Apple did away with Touch Id and replaced it with facial ID for quicker access. The most recent Apple iPad model, which has an A14 processor, is as quick as a Mac using an Intel processor. In order to improve saturation and brightness, Apple also concentrated on speeding up the refresh rate and offering a stunning OLED-like display. The second-generation Apple Pencil, which is a superior stylus to the first-generation Apple Pencil, is also supported with these iPad Pro models. There are various sizes available for each of these Apple iPad models.

Newest iPad Air (2020): Professionals who don't want a high-quality screen can also choose from one of Apple's mid-tier Air options. The iPad Air has a sleek appearance and a powerful A14 CPU. It can also be charged through USB-C, making it a great long-term gadget.

IPad from Apple with M1 processor (2021): The most recent iPad model includes the same M1 CPU found in all of Apple's newest Mac computers. The M1 chip is three times faster than the Apple A14 processor and six times faster than Android tablets. The more recent Apple iPad can render sophisticated machine learning models quickly and enables high-level augmented reality apps. It is the finest option Apple has right now to provide its customers.

Basic terminology about main functions

Although this book is intended for laypeople without any prior knowledge of the Apple iPad, we nevertheless want you to be able to understand some of the basic terms used in order for you to fully appreciate the information presented.

Apple Ecosystem: As an American firm, Apple offers a variety of services and products to its customers. Apple's well-integrated ecosystem ensures that you can access other Apple devices concurrently and almost instantaneously. For instance, you can email files instantly from your iPad to iPhone. Following an ecosystem offers benefits and drawbacks.

Hardware: The components that enable your iPad to function as intended are known as hardware. Some of the hardware elements found in an iPad include the processor, screen, buttons, metal body, and speakers.

Operating System (OS): An operating system serves as a communication channel between a user and a device. No other operating system may be installed on an iPad; iPad OS is the device's default operating system.

App Store: The iPad comes preloaded with a number of apps, but you can add a ton more by utilizing the App Store. Think of it as an iPad "mall" where you can purchase and install various apps (apps). The App Store offers both paid and unpaid apps. The App Store currently hosts more than 2 million programs.

Apps: Applications are a type of software for mobile or portable devices. An illustration of an application would be the iPad version of Maps. The objectives of various applications vary.

iCloud: Apple's users are given access to iCloud by default as their cloud manager. With iCloud, you can put all of your photos, movies, documents, and app data on Apple's cloud servers without ever having to worry about losing them. With the aid of iCloud, data synchronization across several devices is simple. In the later chapters of the book, we shall discuss how iCloud functions.

Browser: Software that allows you to browse the internet is referred to as a browser. On the iPad, the built-in browser is Safari, but you can also download other browsers from the App Store, including Google Chrome and Firefox.

Apple ID: This is the default ID that Apple requests from you in order to use various Apple services, including iCloud. You can hardly use your iPad to its full potential without an Apple ID.

Siri: All Apple devices come with Siri preinstalled by default. With Siri, voice instructions are a simple way to operate an iPad.

Storage: Each iPad has a certain amount of default storage that may be used to store applications, multimedia files, and application data. In addition to the iPad's default storage, you can also use iCloud storage to meet your storage demands.

Home screen: Your home screen is the desktop on your own computer. Your device will launch to the home screen when you restart it or hit the touch ID button on your iPad.

Wi-Fi/Cellular: In terms of internet access, there are two different iPad models: Wi-Fi and cellular. Unlike cellular versions, which also allow you to connect to your iPad via mobile data, Wi-Fi iPads can only be connected to Wi-Fi networks.

iPad Camera

These days, the camera is a necessary piece of hardware for every gadget. While the first iPad, which was released in 2010, lacked a camera, the second generation, which was released in 2011, had both front and rear cameras. Since then, users of iPads have had access to two excellent cameras. Although the lenses on iPad cameras are not as good as those on iPhones, they still have excellent cameras. You must be aware of several options if you want to use the camera app to shoot better pictures and movies.

To use your camera, go to the home screen and select the camera app.

You may also use the "Hey Siri! open the camera" command to ask Siri to do something.

Understanding Photos App

iPad cameras are powerful and allow you to take photos in different photo formats such as JPEG, PNG, and TIFF. iPads inbuilt camera supports square or panorama mode. Higher-end models such as iPad pro also support portrait mode for better quality pictures.

With iPad, it is also easy to edit your pictures once taken and share them on different social media platforms or directly into your gallery. The photo-sharing feature and Apple's constant update process to iCloud also make it easy for individuals to make sure their photos are available across all their devices.

All your photos and videos taken by the camera will be present in the "Photos" app for you to look at. These photos will also be categorized and divided into Albums for easier access. You can also create your custom albums for managing your Photo library efficiently.

Taking Pictures With iPad Cameras

To make use of your camera, click on the "Camera" app on the screen.

In the bottom right of the screen, you will be able to select the mode for your camera such as video, photo, slo-mo, time-lapse, square, and pano. Depending on the iPad you are using, options may vary.

Make sure that this option is on "Photo" for you to take high-quality photographs with your iPad. You can use autofocus or flash to enhance your pictures.

Once you have set the "Photo" option, click on the big circle on the screen to take a photograph. The photo will be immediately saved to your "Photos" app.

Taking Videos With the iPad Camera

iPads also provide powerful cameras to take cinematic and portrait videos. Right now, only iPad Pro models provide cinematic quality for your videos. All the other iPads offer high definition (HD) quality videos for the users.

To start taking videos with your iPad, you should first select the video mode in your camera app. Just swipe down in the camera menu and you will enter the video mode.

When you are in video mode, the middle circle button becomes red. It is a good sign to find out whether you are almost instantly in camera or video mode.

- You can now click on the red button for the video to start recording.

- On the top screen you will be able to see how much time it has been recorded.

- You can use a pinch gesture with your fingers to zoom in or out. You can also use volume up and down buttons to zoom in or out using your camera.

- When the recording is completed, you can click on the "stop" button for the video to stop.

Your video file will be automatically saved to your "Photos" app.

How to Use Live Text?

- To use the live text feature, you need to use the camera app as usual.

- When the text is detected, it will show a yellow frame around it. You can now click on the icon that looks like a few lines between the camera to use it for live text features.

- Once the text is selected, you can either copy, translate, or share them by swiping the text.

Chapter 2: How to setup iPad for the first time

Getting Started: How to Set up the iPad

You can set up the iPad over an internet connection or by connecting it to your computer. You can transfer data to your new iPad from your iPad, iPhone, iPod touch or even an Android device.

Note: if a school, company, or organization manages or deployed the iPad for you, you will need to meet with the teacher or administrator for setup instructions.

Items You Need for Setting Up

For you to have a smooth setup, you need to have the following items available:

Internet connection either via a cellular data service or via a Wi-Fi network. You will need the name and password if the network is protected.

An Apple ID user name and password, if you do not have one already, you can create during the setup process.

Your debit or credit card details if you will like to complete the Apple Pay process during set up.

Back up your old device, if you want to move data to the new device or have the old iPad handy.

An android device if transferring content via android.

Setup your Device

Press and hold down the button at the top until you see the Apple logo on your screen.You will see the "Hello" greeting appear on your screen in multiple languages. You can activate the VoiceOver or Zoom Option on this screen, which is helpful for the blind or those with low vision.

Select your language, then click on your country and region. Ensure to select the right information as it will affect how information like time, date, and more will appear on your device.

You can also click on the blue accessibility button to set up your accessibility options for optimizing your setup experience.

If you want to set up the device manually, click on Set Up Manually, then follow the instructions on your screen to set up your device.

Place the two devices beside each other, then follow the instructions on your screen to securely copy several preferences, settings, and iCloud Keychain from the other device to your new iPad. You can restore the remaining contents and data from the iCloud backup.

Or, if both devices are on iPad later, you can wirelessly transfer all your data from the previous device to your new iPad.

Place both devices beside each other.

Let both devices remain plugged into power until the transfer process finishes.

If you are blind or have low vision, click on the button at the top of your iPad three times to activate VoiceOver, the screen reader.

Now, you have to connect your device to a cellular or Wi-Fi network or iTunes to activate your iPad and continue with the setup. You should have inserted the SIM card before turning on the iPad if going with the cellular network option. To connect to a Wi-Fi network, tap the name of your Wi-fi, and it connects if there is no password on the Wi-fi. If there is a security lock on the Wi-fi, the screen will prompt you for the password before it connects.

Next is to set up your Face ID. The face ID feature gives you access to authorize purchases and unlock your devices. If you want to set up Face ID now, tap Continue and follow the instructions on the screen. You can push this to a later time by selecting "Set Up Later in Settings."

Whether you set up Face ID now or later, you will be required to create a four-digit passcode to safeguard your data. This passcode is needed to access Face ID and Apple Pay. Tap "Passcode Option" to set up a four-digit passcode, custom passcode, or even no passcode.

If you have an existing iTunes or iCloud backup, or even an Android device, you can restore the backed-up data to your new phone or move data from the old device to the new iPad. To restore using iCloud, choose "Restore from iCloud Backup" or "Restore from iTunes Backup" to restore from iTunes to your new iPad. In the absence of any backup or if this is your first device then select "Set Up as New iPad."

To continue, you will need to enter your Apple ID. If you have an existing Apple account, enter the ID and password to sign in. In case you don't have an existing Apple ID or may have forgotten the login details, then select "Don't have an Apple ID or forget it." If you belong to the class that has multiple Apple IDs, then choose "Use different Apple IDs for iCloud & iTunes."

To proceed, you need to accept iOS terms and conditions.

Next is to set up Siri and other services needed on your device. Siri needs to learn your voice, so you will need to speak a few words to Siri at this point. You can also set up the iCloud keychain and Apple Pay at this point.

Set up screen time. This feature will let you know the amount of time you spend on your device. You can also set time limits for your daily app usage.

Now turn on automatic update and other essential features.

Click on "Get Started" to complete the process. And now, you can explore and enjoy your device.

Note: if the iPad doesn't come on, it means you need to charge it before attempting to power it on again.

Move Contents from Android Device to iPad

When setting up your new iPad, you can securely and automatically move data to your iPad from an android device. Please note that the Move to iOS app only works when you are setting up the iPad for the first time. To use this feature after you have completed setup, you will need to erase the iPad and begin anew; otherwise, you will have to move your data manually.

When you first set up your new iPad, you can automatically and securely move your data from an Android device with the steps below:

Connect to Wi-Fi on your Android device.

Ensure that both the android and the new iPad are plugged into power.

Confirm that your new device has enough space to contain the items you want to move. To transfer your Chrome bookmarks, you have to be on the latest Chrome version on your Android device.

Download the 'Move to iOS' app on your android.

Go to your iPad, follow the set-up assistant, then click on Apps & Data screen.

Click on Move Data from Android.

Go to your android device and launch the Move to iOS app.

Click on Continue in the app.

Terms and conditions will appear on the next screen. Read and then click on Agree.

Click on Next in the screen for Find Your Code in the android device.

Go to your iPad device and click on Continue in the screen for Move from Android.

You will receive a 6- or 10-digit code on your iPad screen. If you receive an alert of weak connection from your Android, ignore the warning.

Input the displayed code into the Android device, and then you will see the screen for Transfer Data.

Select the contents you want to move from your Android device then click on Next.

Even if you receive a notification on your android that the process is complete, it is best to leave both devices until you see that the loading bar on your iPad is full. It can take some time to complete the transfer, usually dependent on the size of the contents you are moving.

The contents that you can transfer include messages, contacts, camera videos and photos, history, web bookmarks, calendars and mail accounts. When the transfer is complete, you can redownload all the free apps matched from the app store.

When the loading bar on the iPad gets full, go to your android device and click on Done.

Then click on Continue on your iPad and follow the steps in the setup guide above to complete the setup process.

Transfer Data Using Quick-Start Option from the Previous iOS to your iPad

You can move contents and data from your previous iPod, or iPad to your most recent device. Quick Start allows you to quickly set up your new device using data from the previous one. When using Quick Start, you may be unable to do any other thing on both devices, so you must perform this process when you do not need to make use of your devices.

Power on your iPad and position it close to your previous device.

The QuickStart screen will appear on the screen of your old device while setting up the new iPad with the option to set up your new iPad using Apple ID.

Confirm the Apple ID is the right one before you click on Continue.

If you cannot find the option for Continue on your old device, ensure your Bluetooth is activated.

Allow some seconds for an animation to show on your new device.

Hold your old device over the new iPad and position the animation to fit into the viewfinder.

You will receive a message on the screen reading, Finish on New [Device].

If you do not want to make use of the camera in your current device, click on Authenticate Manually and follow the instructions you will see on your screen.

When asked, input the passcode for the current device into the new iPad.

Follow the instructions on your new iPad to set up Face ID or Touch ID.

Input the Apple ID on your iPad when prompted.

Your new iPad will give you options for restoring data, apps, and settings from the last iCloud backup or to first update backup on your current device before reinstalling on the new one. Choose your preferred option and then select whether you want to transfer some settings related to privacy, location, Siri and Apple Pay.

Ensure that you are connected to a strong Wi-Fi network before you update backup on your device.

Restart your iPad

Press and hold down the button at the top of your device along with any of the volume button until you see the power off slider on your screen

Drag the slider to the right to turn off your device.

Press and hold down on the top button again to power on the device. Hold down until you see the Apple logo.

Download iPad

To be able to enjoy the features packed in the iPad, you first have to download it on your iPad. The first step is to back up your iPad to make it easy for you to restore your device if you lose your content during the upgrade.

Backup Using iCloud

The step below is probably the simplest way to back up your device.

Connect your device to a Wi-Fi network.

Go to the settings app.

Click on your name at the top of the screen.

Then click on iCloud.

Navigate down and click on iCloud backup.

Then select Back Up Now.

To confirm the status of the backup, follow the steps below

Go to settings.

Click on iCloud.

Then select iCloud BackUp.

Navigate to iCloud Backup, and there you will see the time and date of your last backup.

Back Up on MacOS Catalina

Connect your iPad device to the Mac and ensure its updated.

Follow the instructions on the screen and enter your passcode if requested or activate the Trust This Computer option.

Launch the Finder App.

Choose your iPad device from the sidebar.

Click on General.

Then click on Back Up Now to begin a manual backup.

<u>Back Up with iTunes on PC or Mac</u>

if you have a Windows PC or an older Mac, you can use iTunes to back up your iPad with the steps below:

Confirm that the iTunes is updated to the current version, then launch iTunes and connect your iPad to the PC.

Follow the instructions on the screen and enter your passcode if requested or activate the Trust This Computer option.

In the iTunes app, click on your iPad.

Then click on Back Up Now to back up your device.

To confirm that the backup was successful, navigate to Latest Backup to see the date and time of the last backup.

<u>Download and Install iPad / iOS 13 on your iPad</u>

The best way to download iOS 13 on your iPad is via air with the steps below:

Go to the settings app.

Click on General.

Then select Software Update.

Your device will begin to search for a new update, after which you will receive notification of the ipad.

Click on Download and Install.

It may take a while to download, and you will not be able to make use of your device during the update.

Download and Install iPad on PC or Mac Through iTunes

If you will instead download the iPad to your PC or Mac through iTunes, use the highlighted steps below:

You have to be on the most current version of iTunes.

Connect the iPad to your computer.

Launch iTunes then click on your iPad.

On the next screen, select Summary.

Then click on Check for Update.

Finally, click on Download and Update.

Hard reset your iPad Device

Most challenges you encounter with your device can be resolved by restarting your iPad. However, the normal restart process may not always work. There are times you may not even see the slider and the iPad will refuse to respond to touch. In cases like these, a hard reset is needed. This step will not clear data from your phone, but will only delete the memory for the operating system and apps. The steps below will show you how to perform a hard reset:

Press the Volume Up button and quickly release it.

Press the Volume Down button and quickly release it.

Then press down the Power button and hold until your device restarts.

How to Erase Your iPad Settings and Data

You can choose to delete some specific settings from your device or restore the iPad back to default factory settings. A factory reset will erase every data stored on your iPad and return the device to its original form. Every single data from settings to personal data saved on the iPad will be deleted. It is important you create a backup before you go through this process. Once you have successfully backed up your data, please follow the steps below to wipe your iPad.

From the Home screen, click on Settings.

Click on General.

Select Reset.

Choose the option that suits what you need:

For factory reset, select Erase All Content and Settings. This option will return the iPad to its original state from the store.

Click on Reset All Settings if you want to reset just your settings without erasing your apps and data.

When you click on Reset Network Settings, it will restore your wireless network settings to factory default.

Reset Keyboard Dictionary option will delete all the spellings and words you added to your device's spellchecker/ dictionary.

Reset Home Screen Layout option will disable all the arrangements of apps and folders you have and return the home screen layout to default.

Reset Location and Privacy option will delete all the permissions on your device, and then the apps will have to request for the permission again.

When asked, enter your passcode to proceed.

Click Erase iPad to approve the action.

Depending on the volume of data on your iPad, it may take some time for the factory reset to complete. Once done with the reset, you may choose to set up using the iOS Setup Assistant/Wizard, where you can choose to restore data from a previous iOS or proceed to set the device as a fresh one.

Cycle Tracking

The health app in the Apple device is a great tool, and iOS 13 has brought more additions, including cycle tracking. With this tool, you can track your menstrual cycle and also have tools to alert you when you are at your most fertile days, and when you are due. To get started, follow the steps below:

Launch the health app.

Then choose Search, and click on Cycle tracking from the displayed list.

Click on Get started, then click on Next.

The app will ask you a series of questions like the duration of your period and the date of the last cycle.

You will also have to choose the ways you will like to track your period, whether you want to receive notifications and predictions on your next cycle, if you will like to record spotting and symptoms in your cycle log and if you wish to be able to view your fertility Windows.

As soon as you have provided all the answers, you will return to the homepage for Cycle Tracking.

On this screen, click on Add Period to choose days that you have experienced your periods.

You can also click on Spotting, Symptoms, and Flow Levels option to input more specific details.

Find My App

In iOS 13, Apple combined the Find My iPhone and Find My Friends feature into an app they called Find My. With this feature, you can share your location with your loved ones and friends and also find your missing devices. It is simple to use with the steps below

Go to your home page and launch the Find My app.

Under the People tab, you will see your current location.

Click on the Start Sharing Location tab to share your location with another user.

Type in the name of the contact that you want to send the location update.

To find your missing device,

Click on the Device tab to modify your map to present all the registered Apple devices on your account.

Click on the missing device then select from any of the options on the screen: Mark As Lost, Get Directions to the device, remotely Erase This Device, or Play Sound.

If any of the devices are currently offline, you can set the map to alert you once the device gets connected to the internet by clicking the Notify Me option.

Network and Communication

Unlike 20 years ago, the world is now connected like a spiderweb with the help of the internet. The internet is also filled with websites that help people do practically anything they want. You can order a dress or watch an old movie or play a game with your buddies with the help of the internet. IPad, as a device, is capable of doing countless things that the internet offers for the users. Learn about some of the different ways to use the web and communicate with your loved ones or acquaintances using the basics covered for you in this chapter.

How Will your iPad Access the Internet?

IPad uses its Wi-Fi or cellular capability to connect to the internet. Even when you are first setting up your device, an internet connection is mandatory for Apple to check the authenticity of your device. So, if you don't have Wi-Fi or a mobile data-enabled device, then your device will not start functioning as intended.

What Is Wi-Fi?

Wi-Fi is a network facility that helps devices connect to the network wirelessly. All you need is a Wi-Fi connection from your nearby network service provider and a router to use Wi-Fi for several devices such as your smartphone, iPad, and computer. There are also many public hotspots worldwide that allow you to access the internet for free or for a nominal fee.

What Is Cellular Data?

Cellular data is a network facility where you can access the internet with the help of the SIM card or by an active mobile connection you are using on your device. iPads with cellular data support usually cost more than the Wi-Fi-enabled iPads.

How to Connect to the Internet

To connect to the internet, head over to Settings > Wi-Fi, or Settings > Mobile Data and connect to your home or mobile network. To verify whether or not your network connection is active, you can open the App Store. If the App Store opens without any problems, your internet connection is active.

To get the most out of the internet, you need browsers to visit different websites. All modern browsers use complex frameworks to quickly parse web pages and provide them to the end-user intuitively.

Safari, the browser developed by Apple, is one of the smoothest and most visually appealing browsers available right now for internet users. Safari is exclusive to Apple devices and a native app for iPad users.

How to Browse the Web

Browsing the web on Safari is fun as it has a great Graphical User Interface (GUI) and a lot of options for the users to get the most out of their web experience. You will see a list of icons and text fields on the browser on the top of the screen, and each of them has a specific functionality.

The icon that looks like a book is used to expand the Safari settings and tab details

The buttons that look like less than (<) and greater than (>) symbols both take you to the previous and next page.

When you tap on the "aA" button, you will be able to enter into the reader view, or you can increase or decrease the font size of the web page text.

In the text field you can enter the Uniform Resource Locator (URL)—web address—of the website you want to visit.

The button that looks like a half-circle can be used to reload your webpage.

With the share button that looks like a mail icon, you can easily share your web page link or add it to a bookmark list. There is also an option to print the page easily.

When you click the "+" button, a new tab can be opened on the browser.

The last icon with four boxes can help you to quickly shift between different tabs that are opened in your browser.

You can change several settings for Safari according to your liking. Head over to Settings > Safari and change some of the settings mentioned below for better browsing abilities.

Set the default search engine to Google as it is much better than its rivals (such as Bing).

Toggle on the "Block Pop-ups" option to block any pop-ups while browsing the web.

Verify or change the default file location for your website downloads.

Click on the "Extensions" option to look at the extensions you have installed for Safari. You can easily search different extensions for Safari using the App Store.

Toggle on the "Prevent Cross-site Tracking" option for additional encryption while browsing.

Browsing History

It is easy to track your browsing history with Safari, even if it is a month old. All your records will automatically be synced to your iCloud account, making it easy for you to go back into your recently-visited web pages from the other devices.

To view your recent history during the session, click and hold the previous page button to get recently-visited web pages. Just tap on them to see them.

To view your history more comprehensively, click on the top-left icon and tap on the "History" option. You will now be able to see your browsing history from more than a week before.

If you want to delete the history, click on the "Clear" button.

Search

Safari provides an inbuilt search feature for iPad users to make use of. Usually, by default, Google is the default search engine for all iPad users. Go to the address field and enter any search term for the browser to detect your queries and provide search suggestions.

If you are not satisfied with the search suggestions, click on the "Go" button present on the onscreen keyboard to open a Google search results page.

Bookmarks

Bookmarks act as an easy way to save your favorite web pages in your browser and visit them any way you want.

How to Create a Bookmark:

To create a bookmark for any web page, click on the share button that looks like an upward-pointing arrow on the browser. It will open a pop-up interface, where you need to click the "Add Bookmark" button.

Immediately, you will be taken to another pop-up interface where you can edit the bookmark name for you to easily revisit it after. Once edited, click on the "Save" button to save the bookmark into your browser and iCloud.

You can now click on the tab on the top left to visit your bookmarks any time you want to.

You can also organize bookmarks into folders in this section. There is also an option to delete bookmarks that you no longer need.

Apart from bookmarks, you can also use reading lists to save web pages temporarily. Just click on the share button and click on the "Add to Reading list" button. After reading, you can mark the list item as "Read" for it to disappear from your reading list.

Private Browsing

Private browsing, also known as incognito mode, helps iPad users surf the web anonymously. While not to be confused with Virtual Private Networks (VPN), using the private browsing option doesn't stop your Internet Service Providers (ISPs) or governments from tracking you. Private browsing, however, makes sure that no cookies or log-in details are saved in the browser.

To start using private browsing, click on the "Show/Hide tab" icon on the top left screen, and click on the "Private Browsing" option. You can now click on the "+" button to open a new private tab. Remember that no search history will be saved when you are in private browsing mode.

Download Files

iPad made it easy for Safari users to download files into the iCloud and iPad file manager. First of all, head over to Settings > Downloads and choose a location that you want to use.

To download any files, you first have to click the link on the website, and the browser will automatically redirect a pop-up for you. Click on the "Allow" button on the pop-up for the download to start.

Link Preview

Apple makes it easy to preview any web page before clicking on it. This feature can help you avoid spam pages that can load malware onto your device. To preview a page, click and hold the link for a pop-up to arise where you can see a part of the web page.

Apart from these features, newer versions of Safari can also detect any trackers that are present on websites.

Contacts

Saving contacts is essential for accessible communication. iPads provide a Contacts app for users to add, edit, or delete contacts in their device. All your contacts will be automatically synced to your iCloud account, making it easy for you to have the contact information on different devices almost instantly.

Tap on the Contacts app on the home screen to edit and personalize information.

How to Create a Contact:

To create a new contact in your device, click on the "+" button on the screen when you first open the Contacts application.

A pop-up will arise where you can add details such as first name, second name, company, phone number, email, social profiles, and other additional information for the contact. You can also add details about your relationship with the contact in the "related name" column. You can also add a photograph if you want to for the contact.

Once added, you can change the contact details anytime by tapping on the "Edit" button. However, you can also remove the contact's details by tapping on the "Delete" button that is present at the lower bottom of the screen.

Chapter 4: FaceTime

FaceTime makes it easy for iPad users to stay in touch with their family and friends irrespective of the Apple device they are using. FaceTime is an exclusive Apple video chatting application that makes communication seamless for people who want to stay in touch. FaceTime video calling quality is also one of the best in the industry and is highly encrypted, making it one of the premium features for your iPad.

Communication becomes more immersive and expressive with the latest spatial audio technology introduced in iPad. The newest iPad versions also provide SharePlay to make it easy for people to watch movies or listen to music together while in a FaceTime call.

To get the most out of the FaceTime in your iPad, head over to Settings>FaceTime and turn on the FaceTime feature.

When you turn on the FaceTime feature on your iPad, it will use your Apple ID to connect to the FaceTime application. Click on the "Use Apple ID" option present in the same interface to enter your Apple ID password.

If you use a cellular iPad, your mobile number can also be used to reach you on FaceTime.

How to Make FaceTime Calls

You need another person's Apple ID or mobile number to make a FaceTime call.

Head over to the FaceTime application and click on "New FaceTime" to add a number or email address.

Once done, click on the FaceTime icon or Audio button to start a video or voice call.

You can also add multiple numbers to make a Group FaceTime.

While in a FaceTime call, you can use SharePlay to watch movies or listen to music together. You can also use animated emojis while talking with your friends and family.

iMessage

iMessage is one of the few messaging apps restricted to only a particular system. While traditional messaging apps like WhatsApp and telegram rule the Android space, Apple users are already equipped with a well-functioning messaging platform in the form of iMessage. You can use both Wi-Fi and cellular service to use it from your device.

iMessage is the default messaging app for your device. As iMessage is exclusively available for Apple devices, if the other party in the transaction doesn't have an Apple device, your message will be sent to them as a Short Message Service (SMS) or Multimedia Message Service (MMS) message.

All your messages are highly encrypted, and hence iMessage boasts its privacy features.

How to Sign In to iMessage

To sign in to iMessage, make sure that you are logged in with your Apple ID, or that your mobile number is active if it is a cellular iPad.

Go to Settings>Messages and turn on the "iMessage" option.

If you log in with the same Apple ID on different devices, all of your messages will automatically be synced and reflected on those devices.

How to Send and Receive Messages

With the Messages app, you can send text messages, photos, videos, Memojis, and audio messages. iMessage is a fun application, and provides opportunities to send messages with animated effects, and many other premium options for Apple iPad users.

With iMessage, you can send a text message to one or more people at the same time.

Click on the icon with a pen on the top of the screen to create a new message. If there is an existing conversation, you can click on it to send a message.

In the "To" section, enter the numbers or contact names to whom you are trying to send the message.

After choosing the contacts, head over to the text field and enter your text message. After completing the message, click on the arrow button with a blue arrow mark to send your message to the recipient.

In the same way, you can respond to messages by tapping on a particular conversation and entering the text field. You can also use emojis whenever you want from the keyboard.

While in the Messages app you also can press on the FaceTime icon to create a video call with the contact at any time.

How to Send Attachments

The iMessage app makes it easy to send photos and videos with just a click. Just click on the camera icon to take a new photo, or choose one or many images from the iPad. Once added, click on the blue arrow button to send these attachments.

In iPad and Air models, you can use the inbuilt Camera app to send photos with filters and Memojis.

How to Send Audio Messages

Audio messages can be a great way to convey a long message with just a few seconds of speech. In the iMessage app, if you want to send a voice message to contacts, hold the icon that looks like waves before your "Send" button. It will record the message. You can click "x" anytime during this recording to stop sending the message. Once the recording is completed, click on the blue arrow button to send it.

By going to Settings>Messages, you can select the time at which these audio messages can expire.

How to Animate Messages

The iMessage app provides breathtaking animated effects for all of your messages. You can also send handwritten messages with the help of the digital feature provided.

Turn your iPad to landscape mode and swipe the menu above the keyboard to use these animated messages or full-screen effects. Tap on the respective unique animated feature you want to try and click the blue arrow to send it to the recipient.

iMessage Apps

Apple also provides access for third-party application developers to create exclusive content such as sticker packs and easy link sharing via iMessage apps. For example, if you have Spotify installed on your iPad, you will unlock the feature to share any Spotify songs directly to your contacts via iMessage.

Like the animated effects feature, you need to first swipe above the onscreen keyboard and select one of the iMessage apps to explore its features.

Memojis

Memojis are an advanced version of emojis. They are interactive and can help you bond or have fun with your closest people. You can create personalized Memojis to send to your family and friends. If using iPad models, you can animate emoji stickers by recording your voice and using a real-depth camera to mirror your facial expressions.

Send or Receive Money

If you have Apple Pay installed and you have saved your cards to it, then you can easily send money from the iMessage app itself by clicking on the Apple Pay button in the iMessage app.

Once in the iMessage app, you can select the amount you would like to send, along with your authentication details. Once verified, your money is immediately sent to the recipient's bank account.

Mail

Electronic mail — or emai l— is one of the popular ways to communicate with people worldwide. Businesses all around the world use email as a preferable way to connect their employees and contact their customers.

Apple provides an inbuilt Mail application for iPad users to easily send, receive, or read new email. You can link any email accounts such as GMail, Yahoo Mail, or Rediff mail to this application.

Go to Settings>Mail and click on the "Add Account" button to add the email account of your favorite service.

How to Check Your Mail

Click on the Mail app and head over to "Inbox," present on the top left of the app. You will be able to read all of the new mail that you have received. Unread emails will usually have a small blue dot beside them. When you read them, these dots will disappear.

How to Send Emails

To send a new email, click on the last icon that looks like a note on the top right of the Mail app.

A new pop-up will arise where you can enter the recipient's email address, your message, and any attachments you may want to add. Once written, click on the blue arrow button to send the email.

To add attachments, just click on the photo icon and add any images or videos to your message.

WhatsApp

WhatsApp is a popular messaging app for iPads. WhatsApp is owned by Facebook and can help you easily communicate with your friends who use an Android phone. While the native messages app is a great communication app for iPad users, it is however exclusive to Apple devices.

Go to the App Store and search "WhatsApp" on the search tab to download WhatsApp to your device. Once downloaded, you need to verify your mobile number with the one time password received.

You can click on the "+" button to start a new conversation with contacts from your device. WhatsApp provides stickers for more interactive communication. All your messages are end-to-end encrypted, making all the communications secure.

Creating Accounts in Social Media Networks

As said before, social media networking apps such as Instagram, Facebook, and TikTok are all accessible from your iPad. To open an account with any app, go to the App Store and search for the app. Once you have found the app, click on the "Get" button to download it to your device.

Now, head over to the home screen and click on the app you have downloaded. All these applications will start with a start screen where you have to either log in to your account or sign up for one. Click on the "Signup" button to create an account for the respective platform.

Enter your basic details such as name, mobile number, address, and age for creating a new account. You may have to verify your identity via email or mail. Once verified, your account will be created, and you can now use the "Login" to enter into the app and explore the possibilities they provide.

ICloud

iCloud keeps your pictures, videos, docs, backups, etc. secure and automatically updated on all your devices. iCloud would give you 5 GB of free storage & an email account. You can sign up with iCloud + for more storage & features.

Change your iCloud settings:

Enter the Settings application> [your name]> iCloud.

Do any of the below:

Check the status of your iCloud storage.

Activate the applications & features you plan on making use of, like mail, pictures, messages, & contacts.

Setup iCloud Drive on iPad.

Utilize the Files application to save files & folders on iCloud Drive.

Activate iCloud Drive:

Enter the settings application, tap on (your name), touch iCloud, and activate iCloud Drive.

Select which applications utilize iCloud Drive.

Enter the Settings application> [your name]> iCloud, then activate or deactivate every application list under iCloud Drive.

Browse iCloud Drive:

In the Files application,

Click the "Browse" button at the lower part of your display.

Under Location, touch iCloud Drive.

If you can't find Locations, touch Browse once more. If you can't find iCloud Drive in Locations, touch Location.

Click on a folder to open it.

Upgrade, change or cancel your iCloud + subscription:

Enter the Settings application> [your name]> iCloud.

Click on Manage Storage, touch change the Storage Plan, then choose an option & adhere to the directives on your display.

Note: If you cancel your iCloud + subscription, you will not be able to access the additional iCloud storage.

Apple Pay

You can use Apple Pay for easy & safe payments in applications & sites.

Add a debit or credit card:

Click on the Setings app icon to open it, then click on Wallet and Apple Pay.

Touch the Add Cards button.

Carry out any of the below:

Add a new card: insert your card's info manually or place your iPad in a way that it can be seen clearly in the frame on your screen.

Add old cards: choose a card that has been used with your Apple ID before or a card you removed. Touch the Continue button, and insert the CVV number for the card.

View the info for a card & change the card's settings.

Navigate to the Settings app, then click on Wallet and Apple Pay.

Touch a card, then carry out any of the below:

Touch Transaction to checkout your history.

Remove the card.

Check the Device Account Number & the last 4 digits of the card number.

Make changes to the billing address.

Change your Apple Pay settings:

Click on the Setings app icon to open it, then click on Wallet and Apple Pay.

Carry out any of the below:

Enter the contact info for purchase & shipping address.

Set the default card.

Make payments with Apple Pay.

You can buy things with Apple Pay in Application Clips, applications, and anywhere the Apple Pay button can be found online.

When checking out, touch the Apple Pay button.

Go through the payment details.

You can make changes to any of the details.

Verify with Touch ID or enter your pass code.

Chapter 5: Graphic design with ipad and apple pencil setup and use

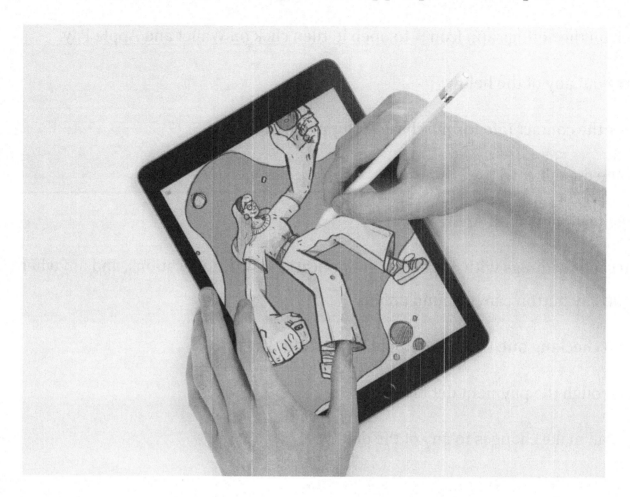

Using Apple Pencil with your iPad

The Apple pencil gives you opportunities to perform several functions on your iPad, from putting your signature to a document to sketching and drawing. Thankfully, the iPad supports the 2nd generation Apple Pencil.

Create a New Note with Apple Pencil on Lock Screen:

If you are looking for a quick way to create a new note, follow the steps below:

The first step is to wake your device.

Then use the Apple pencil to click on your screen.

A new note will appear on your screen instantly.

To reposition the markup toolbar, drag it to any edge.

Create a Signature with the Apple Pencil:

From the bottom corner of your device screen, swipe all the way up.

Click on the Plus (+) sign in the Markup Toolbar.

Select Signature.

On the popup field, sign your name.

Click on Done after you have inputted your signature.

The next time you need to input your signature, you will not have to sign it again.

All you need do is to click on the Plus (+) sign in the Markup toolbar of every app that supports this feature.

Then click on Signature.

Sketch and Draw with the Apple Pencil

This is quite easy. The Apple Pencil allows you to markup, draw, and write with apps from the App store as well as inbuilt apps. Some apps like Notes will allow you to sketch and draw with the Apple Pencil.

The iPad comes with a redesigned tool palette. Move the palette around the screen or minimize it if you want more space to sketch and draw. Use the ruler tool to make straight lines, then use your fingers to rotate them. If you made any mistakes, you can either erase by pixel or by object. To write and draw with your Apple pencil, position your palm on the screen display without it registering like a mark. Increase your hand pressure when drawing thicker lines. To shade, tilt your pencil.

Pair Your Apple Pencil with Your iPad

Fix the apple pencil into the magnetic connector on the side of your iPad.

Unpair Your Apple Pencil with Your iPad

Each time you pair your Apple pencil with your device, it stays paired until you turn on Airplane Mode, restart your device, or pair the Apple pencil to another iPad device.

Sketch or Draw in the Notes App

Open the Note app.

Click on ☑ to begin a new note.

Click on Ⓐ to draw. If you do not find the symbol, you will need to update your Notes app. Click on Ⓐ to sketch.

Then begin to sketch or draw.

Select from the different colors and drawing tools.

Whenever you make a mistake, switch to an eraser to clean it.

Double click on the eraser to see the options for erasing on your device.

Press your pencil firmly on your screen to darken a line or tilt to shade a line.

Note: you can now draw on any part of your screen without activating the Notification Center, Control Center, or Multitasking mistakenly.

Double Clicking your Apple Pencil

With your second-generation Apple pencil, double click on the lower part of the pencil for a fast switch back to the tool that you used last. If you wish to change what happens when you double click the lower part of the pencil, follow the steps below:

Go to Settings

Click on Apple Pencil.

Then select between any of the four options below:

"Show color palette."

"Switch between current tool and last used."

"Switch between current tool and eraser."

"Off"

Charging Your Apple Pencil

The first step is to put on your Bluetooth.

Then fit in your pencil to the magnetic connector in the middle of your iPad close to the right side.

To know how much time is left for the pencil to fully charge, go to the widget's view on your device.

Note: When using your iPad to charge your Apple Pencil and your car's keyless entry device (key fob) is close by, the signal interference may not allow you to unlock the vehicle with the key fob. When you encounter this, distance the key fop from the iPad or even remove the pencil from the iPad and keep aside. Once the Pencil is fully charged, you will notice that all the signal interference will stop.

Troubleshooting Your Apple Pencil

Ensure that the Apple Pencil is well placed on the magnetic connector to the right side of the iPad.

Restart your iPad device before you attempt to pair it again.

Check that Bluetooth is enabled. Go to Settings then click on Bluetooth.

On that same screen, go to the section for My Devices and look for your Apple Pencil.

When you locate your pencil, click on ⓘ.

Then click on Forget this Device.

Plug in the Apple Pencil to the iPad and then click on the Pair button after a few seconds.

If the Pair button does not appear, allow some seconds for the Apple Pencil to charge. Then connect the pencil again and wait for the Pair button to show up.

If the pair button still does not show up, then you will need to contact Apple Support.

Using the Apple Map

I know that the Apple map has been available for some time now, but not so many users fancied it on the older software. Good news is that IOS 13 has brought an improvement to the Apple map to include more beaches, roads, buildings and other details that may interest you. There are other cool features newly added to the Apple map, like being able to add a location to your list of Favorites. You can also arrange the saved places in your personally customized collections. Follow the steps below to add a favorite on the map.

Search for a location or tap on a location.

Scroll down to the bottom and click on Add to Favorites.

You can always access your favorites list on your main page.

To add a particular location to your customized collection,

Drag up from the Apple map's main page.

Then click on My Places.

Select Add a Place.

On the next screen, you can now add any location that you recently viewed to your collection or search through your search bar for the location.

To begin a new collection,

Navigate back to your apple map's main page.

Swipe from the bottom of the screen upwards.

Then click on New Collections to make a new list.

Look Around Feature in Apple Map

Look around is Apple's version of the Streetview from Google as it allows you to preview a location before you visit. Follow the steps below on how to use it.

Search for a location of your choice on the Apple map. Then select it by pressing long on the map.

If the location supports Look around, you will find a look around image on that spot.

Click on it to move down to Street level and drag to navigate around.

While on this view, you can also see facts about the place or even add it to your favorites list by swiping up from the bottom of the screen.

At the moment, Apple hasn't covered all the locations in the USA, but they have promised it do this by end of 2019 and also follow suit for other countries.

Mark Up Pages with the Apple Pencil

To take a screenshot of a page or to annotate it with the Apple pencil, use the Apple pencil to swipe in from the bottom side of your screen.

Reading On an iPad

Books have been the primary source of knowledge for humans for thousands of years. Even with the advancement of different mediums for people to understand, books are still the most intriguing way to recharge your conscious mind. The iPad can act as a splendid reading device compared to laptops and desktops because you can place the iPad just like a book on your palm. Even though iPads are not total e-readers like Kindle and Nook e-readers, they are still the best electronic device to read books, newspapers, magazines, and comics, with the ability to make annotations and notes as seamlessly as possible. You can also use accessories such as an Apple Pencil to edit documents and books, just like how you can on a paperback book.

How to Buy Books

Apple uses its default book reading application called "Books" to let iPad users read books of different formats. You can download books directly from the Apple Books Store or import from other sources to your "Books" application. The Apple BookStore offers millions of free and paid books for Apple users.

To buy new books, tap on the Books app on the home screen to be taken to the app. You can now click on the "Book Store" tab to buy any free or paid book. You can search from millions of books and audiobooks available for iPhone and iPad users. Click on the "Get" button present beside books to download these books to your library if they are free. If they are paid books, you need to enter your payment information for them to download to your library.

All purchases need an active Apple ID for them to go through. Before buying, make sure that you have looked at the Apple Store preview for users to test whether the book is of desirable quality that works for them.

How to Read Books

Once you have downloaded the book(s), they will be sent to the "Library" tab of the app. Just click on the book cover to open the book in Apple's inbuilt Ebook reader. Remember that by default Apple Books application supports only .epub and .pdf files. If you want to read any document formats other than these, such as .mobi, it is impossible.

Reading Now

This section will display all the books that you are currently reading. It will show progress for each book that you are reading. You can also manage your reading goals and easily track your reading progress from this section.

Library

This section provides all the books and audiobooks that you have either imported or downloaded from the Book Store. You can click on the "Collections" options present on the top of the screen to look at different collections that your books have been divided into. You can also click on the "New Connection" button to create a customized collection of books.

Once you click on a book, you will access the default reader. It has advanced document reading futures, and with time Apple promises to increase the features for Ebook readers.

You can turn the pages by swiping from left to right or from right to left. You can also tap any part of the screen to turn to the next or previous page quickly.

You can adjust the screen brightness by dragging the slider.

You can adjust the font of the book if it is of .ePub format using the "Aa" button.

You can also change the background color for better reading during the night.

You can enable the vertical scrolling option using the toggle button.

You can bookmark any page in the book by clicking on the bookmark icon present on the top left of the screen.

You can select any word or any sentence in the book to create a quick note for it.

Notes App

The Notes app helps iPad users create quick notes, checklists, or write a whole manuscript if you want to. Even though it isn't a robust word processor such as Microsoft Word or Google Docs, it still works efficiently for daily usage.

How to Create a Blank Note

Click on the Notes app on the home screen to open the application. Once in the Notes app, click on the last icon on the top left that looks like a pen on the paper to create a new blank note.

Once the note is created, the first sentence you will add will be the title of the note, which will appear in the Notes library.

How to Format

For any text in the Notes app, you can click on the "Aa" icon just above the keyboard to format the text. You need to select the text you want to format to work as intended.

Once the note is written and formatted, you can click on the "Save" button for the note to be saved.

Advanced Options

Notes app provides advanced features for iPad users to perform various tasks with just a few clicks.

Checklists

Checklists are a great way to organize your tasks. For example, while shopping, you can use these checklists to confirm whether or not you have shopped for particular items.

After tapping on the item, you will add new items to the list. Just click on the enter button to head over to the next item in the list. You can format all the list items using the "Aa" button.

You can tap on the circle beside the checklist to mark it as completed. You can also sort all the completed list items for better viewing. You can click on the circle or marked checklist to reorder the items in the list.

Editing a Table

Tables can be a great way to enter analytical and statistical information into a note.

Click on the icon beside the "Aa" button that looks at a table to create a default "2x2" table. You can further add rows and columns by clicking on the icons present on the table to select whether to create a new row or column.

Drawing and Writing in the Notes App

Click on the icon that looks like a pen on the top of the screen. You will enter into scribble mode to draw or write on the notes app using Apple Pencil.

This section has different markup tools to change your writing color, size, and pattern. You can also use the eraser option to undo any drawings quickly.

If present in split-screen mode, you can drag any pictures or other written text using an Apple Pencil.

Adding Attachments

For better note-taking ability, it is essential to have a way to quickly add different attachments such as photos, videos, or scanned document texts. Apple also makes it easy to add maps or links to other documents and web links right from here.

Click on the "Camera" icon present to add attachments. You can select any photo from the gallery or can use live photos.

Translate

Apple made it easy for iOS users to translate their text from one language to another using the default "Translate" app. The Translate app is available exclusively from iOS15 on. If you are using an iPad OS version below 15, you will not be able to translate your text easily. You can, however, install other third-party translators such as Google Translate from the app store to satisfy your translating needs.

Note: Only less than 20 languages are available to translate. With time, however, additional languages will be added.

Tap on the Translate app to open the application. You can select the languages you want the translation for on the initial screen.

For example, English and Mandarin can be selected to convert your English text to Mandarin script. If you want to convert a Mandarin script to English text, you should choose Mandarin as the source language and English as the destination language.

You can also tap on the microphone symbol present on the bottom of the screen to say a phrase and translate it into another language.

When the translated text appears on the screen, you can utilize four options provided by the app.

You can play the audio translation by tapping on the play icon.

You can save the translation by tapping on the star icon.

You can look up different words in the translation by tapping on the book icon.

You can enlarge the translated text by tapping on the enlarge icon.

The Translate app also provides a conversation mode for iPad users, apart from the translation model. This feature can be helpful when two people with different native languages need to converse in real time.

All you have to do is open the app in conversation mode and tap on the screen for the device to detect your voice and translate it into another language to respond to the app, and it can translate back to you. The iPad will automatically detect your voice from the following conversation without tapping the screen.

News

News is the brand new iPad application that helps iPad users easily explore news from different popular websites from their region from one interface. You can personalize the news articles that will be displayed on the application. At present, the News application is available only in a few regions.

How to Get Personalized Content

To get personalized news articles on your News application, you need to add different channels for your account. You can also search for various topics and add them by clicking on the "+" button.

Apple also provides a new subscription service called Apple News+ to read from hundreds of local and international magazines.

How to Read Stories

Whenever you find a story that you like from the recommendations provided, click on the articles to open in the Apple News inbuilt reader. You can also quickly swipe left or right to go to the next or previous article.

By clicking on the "aA" button you will be able to change the font size settings.

You can easily share the settings by clicking on the icon with three dots.

You can also quickly look at the details of the magazine in which the story was published and look at different issues that are available for you to read.

You can also download these issues to your offline storage to read them without the internet. If the offline issues are no longer needed, you can click on the bin icon to delete them permanently.

Chapter 6: How to get the best from your ipad

Change or turn off sounds

To learn how to change or turn off sounds on the iPad, you need to know a little about the device's design and its internal design. There are two types of speakers, front facing speakers and back facing speakers. With the help of these front facing speakers, you can play music or watch videos. And with the help of back facing speakers, you can use the device for gaming. Now, all these speakers are under the hood of iPad Pro.

To change or turn off sounds on iPad, follow the following steps:

Make a basic settings change

If you have already enabled the USB audio output, you need to make a simple settings change.

Go to Settings and open the General section.

Tap on Sound & Haptics section and you can see the audio output is set to the automatic, so you need to turn it off.

Press and hold the Sleep/Wake button and then press the play button to turn the automatic off.

Make a change to the audio output

Verify whether the audio output in the device is set to the automatic.

Go to Settings and select the General section.

Tap on the Sound & Haptics.

Click on the Output section and you can see there is a symbol there is called Fixed.

Tap and then you can see the audio output is set to Fixed.

Change the audio output with Bluetooth

With the help of Bluetooth, you can connect the speakers to your device. And when the system is connected with the Bluetooth, you can easily change the output mode from fixed to automatic.

Here, you need to tap on the Bluetooth setting and then you can see the output mode is set to Automatic.

Go back to the Settings > General > Sound & Haptic and you can find out that the Bluetooth is set to Bluetooth Enabled.

Tap on the Bluetooth setting and then you can see the output mode is set to Fixed. Now, you need to go back to the Settings and go to the General section and select the Sound & Haptic section. Now, you can see that the Bluetooth is set to the Enabled, and you can change it to the automatic output mode.

Now, you have the automatic output mode to your device. You can easily set the volume and the loudness of the speakers using the remote control or the buttons on the speakers.

Use the Bluetooth remote to adjust the volume

In this step, I will tell you how to use the Bluetooth remote control to change the volume of the speakers.

On the Bluetooth connection page, select the connected Bluetooth from the Bluetooth devices. Now, you need to tap on the connection option and then see the connected Bluetooth devices listed here. Select the connected Bluetooth speakers and then you can see that the connected option is highlighted.

Open apps

You can use the new drag-and-drop feature on your Home screen to open an app. To do this, press and hold down on the app icon on the Home screen and then drag the icon to wherever on the screen you want it to be opened.

When the app opens, it'll appear in the location you've chosen on the Home screen. If you want to drag it to a new location, press and hold down on the app icon and then drag to a new location.

There's also a little arrow icon in the upper left-hand corner of the icon. If you tap on that, it'll bring up a menu that has the option to move the app to the left, right, or the Home screen.

How to take a screenshot or screen recording

To take a screenshot or record a screen video:

Launch any app.

Tap the upper right corner.

A popup menu will appear. Tap "Show keyboard" or "Show system buttons".

Swipe your finger along the right edge to get to the power button.

Tap the power button to turn off the screen and lock the screen. This will take a screenshot.

Press volume down on your keyboard. The volume rocker will act like a button and take a screenshot.

Tap and hold your finger on your iPad screen.

A screenshot will appear in your photo album. You can now choose whether to send it to the photo sharing app or to somewhere else on your device.

Swipe your finger down the display. If you have a lock screen on, you will see "Accessibility Shortcut" appear in your notification center. Tap it to unlock your device.

Tap the picture. The screenshot will be sent to the app.

Tap the picture. A share sheet will appear. You can either share it through your favorite social network or email.

Tap the email button to send the image to an email address.

You can either choose to open the screenshot or save it in your screenshot folder.

Alternatively, you can do a screen recording.

Tap and hold your finger on the screen.

Drag your finger to record a screen video.

You can record a screen video in the Photos app or any other app.

Tap and hold your finger on your iPad screen.

Tap and hold until you see the camera icon.

Record a screen video.

Tap your video on the share sheet to view or save it.

You can also record a video while on a call. Just tap the microphone button to start recording and tap it again to stop.

How to change or lock the screen orientation

You can use the following steps to change the orientation of the iPad screen from any orientation that it is in.

Launch Settings.

Tap General > Accessibility > Rotate, then select the option to change the screen orientation.

If you are unable to change the screen orientation, or there is a message saying that you are in the incorrect orientation, try repeating the above steps

If you do not have any accessibility issues with your iPad, you can skip this step and proceed to the next step.

How to use your apps

You can't download every app that you are familiar with. So how to make sure that you get the most out of your iPad as you go through your day? What kind of apps do you need?

First of all, you should know what apps you need when you travel with your iPad Pro. Here are a few options:

- Gmail

- Slack

- Calendar

- Cards

- Evernote

- Foursquare

- Safari

- Maps

- GitHub

As you can see from the list, there is a wide variety of apps you may want to use your iPad for. Decide which apps are most useful for you, and keep some extra ones for fun, but remember not to clutter your device with too many apps that you rarely use.

How to use multiple apps simultaneously

At first it may look like the multi-tasking on iPad doesn't work at all, but it does. And the secret to using it is Apple's Split View. Let's start by taking a look at the way it works.

Press on one of the icons in the bottom bar, then you see all the app icons in the center. Press on one app to bring it up.

If you double tap the Home button, it will then bring up the multitasking bar. And you can easily swipe back to the last app you were using.

How to annotate documents and images

If you're not familiar with markup, it's just markup language with formatting. You can use markup to alter how your information appears rather than the conventional bullet points, paragraph breaks, and indentation. It can be used for a wide range of formatting options. Although a picture might be included in a bulleted list, the list itself would look different from one without any styling. Additionally, you can use markup to switch out some text for another sort of text, such as a blockquote, a header, or italicized text.

Any program can benefit from using markup pages to display content. Using Markup, you may include dynamic material in your app. For instance, you could design pages that are presented as lists, with the list elements representing various alternatives the user can select from. A page with an article's worth of text, images, links, and a headline can be created using this tool. Additionally, you may make sites for quizzes, polls, and games where you can include questions and answers.

Here are some examples of what Markup can be used for:

Create Pages - A page can be added to your app. The pages you design can be as straightforward or intricate as you choose.

A straightforward page with text and an image can be made. You can also design a page with links, graphics, and a heading for content that is more intricate.

A view controller may be given a Markup page.

Consider that your iPad app has a tab view controller. By creating Markup page objects for each tab, you may add markup pages to your app. You can add a Markup page instance to the tab view controller by creating one in your view controller.

How to take swift action

Using the "Quick Actions" is a rather simple procedure. Use the "Quick Actions" if you need to complete a task quickly. The primary goal of "Quick Actions" is to turn the iOS device into "Quick Access" for a variety of actions or shortcuts, like opening an app, calling a contact, sending a message, accessing a URL, turning on the Wi-Fi, sharing a picture or a file, etc.

First, access "Settings."

Go to "Settings" and select "General."

Open "Quick Actions" in step two.

By clicking the "+" button just above the top right corner of the screen, you can access the "Quick Actions." soon after selecting "Quick Actions."

Select the necessary "Quick Actions".

Use the "Quick Actions" in step four.

Press the "+" button and choose the activities you want to execute to use the "Quick Actions." You can open a contact, send a message, share a file, call a contact, share an image, and more by using the "Quick Actions."

Click "Quick Actions" to carry out the tasks.

By clicking the "+" button, we have already decided which chores we will complete. By selecting "Quick Actions," we can carry out these tasks.

Using and customizing Control Point

The system-level menu for the iPad may be found in the top-right corner. It is called Control Center. It's an easy method to start apps, change Wi-Fi networks, and complete other activities. The iPad has Control Center pre-installed. However, you can alter it to increase its usefulness.

Press the home button to bring up the menu in the top-right corner of the screen before using Control Center.

Steps for adding widgets:

Widget configuration can take several different forms.

On the right top of the screen, click the tiny icon. Look at the screenshot to see.

All widgets will be listed for you to see.

Click and hold the widget you want to customize.

There will be a widget.

You can add a widget by tapping Add widget to add other widgets. A widget will be added and then appear.

How to maintain and charge a battery

An LED status display on the iPad Smart Battery case charger indicates the charging state.

When the iPad is charging, the power button on the charger will become blue.

The iPad is slowly discharged after being charged. Connect the charger to a power source to confirm that it is charging and discharging. A green dot will appear on the LED display when the battery is fully charged.

Traveling with an iPad

An iPad can be used for more than just web browsing, movie streaming, and reading when traveling. You need more than just an iPad and headphones to be productive while traveling with an iPad. To be genuinely productive, you must utilize the features and functions on your iPad Pro.

A charging cable and Lightning-to-USB-C connection for connecting to your MacBook are two of the greatest iPad travel accessories. In a busy airport, a fantastic MacBook charging cable will prevent you from having to search through your suitcase for the iPad adaptor and risk running out of juice just when you need it most.

A power strip with a built-in surge protector is also necessary to shield the gadgets in your luggage from power surges and lightning.

Before leaving the house, cover your iPad with a case to prevent drops and bag scratches. Of course, the iPad won't pass through airport security if you don't have a case or bag. Thus, preparation is necessary, especially if you're traveling abroad. For instance, you could find it difficult to change the battery in your iPad while flying abroad.

If you're carrying an iPad in your bag, take it out before you settle into your seat.

Activate the airplane mode:

Toggle airplane mode in Settings > Wi-Fi to accomplish this.

Tricks and Tips for your iPad

The iPad is a wonderful device designed with the focus of providing value to the consumer. Apple made sure to introduce different simple tricks for the users to enrich their experience with this device. In this chapter we will look at some of the tricks that can help you in different situations.

Take a Screenshot

Taking screenshots is an essential skill that all iPad users need to know. All of the screenshots you take will usually be saved after confirming them, and any unsaved screenshots will automatically be deleted from the internal memory of the iPad.

There are two different ways to take screenshots, depending on the iPad model you are using.

For iPads Without a Home Button:

If you are using an iPad without a home button, you need to press the top button and any volume button simultaneously, and then quickly release them to trigger a screenshot of your entire screen.

For iPads With a Home Button:

If you are using an iPad with a home button, you need to press the top and home buttons simultaneously, and then quickly release them to trigger a screenshot of your entire screen.

Once your screenshot is done, a small thumbnail will appear on the bottom left of the screen. If you don't click on the thumbnail or swipe it, the screenshot will disappear from your iPad.

What Screenshot Options You Have

When you tap on the thumbnail, you will be taken to an interface where you can apply different options to your screenshot.

You can increase the transparency of the screenshot by using the slider provided on the top left of the screen.

You can edit the picture by tapping on the en symbol provided. You can even use an Apple Pencil to make any notes on the image.

In the picture itself, there is a crop option to select only a part of the screenshot.

Once everything is alright with the screenshot, you can click on "Done" to save the screenshot to your photo gallery or files. There is also an option to delete the screenshot, or share the screenshot with other apps.

Measure App

The Measure app makes it easy to gauge the size of real-world objects with the help of augmented reality technology. Newer iPad models use Lidar sensors to ensure that the measurements are as accurate as possible.

So how can you take measurements using the Measure app?

Tap on the Measure app from the app library and follow the onscreen instructions carefully.

The iPad Measure app will usually display a frame of reference on the screen for you to place the surface on it. Keep moving the device until you see a circle with a dot.

After the dot appears, place it on the item you are trying to measure and tap on the "+" button. You have now registered the starting point.

Now move the line to the endpoint where you want to measure and click on the "+" button again.

The app will now measure the distance and provide accurate measurements. Using a rectangle, you can continue the same process to measure other complex systems.

How to Measure a Person's Height Using the Measure App

The newer iPad models have an additional feature of measuring a person's height with the help of portrait mode. Open the Measure app and ensure that the person whose height you are trying to measure is in the viewfinder. Once detected, the app will automatically calculate the person's height and display it on the screen. For accurate measurements, make sure that there is enough light and no reflective surfaces nearby.

Dark Mode

Dark mode is an exclusive system-wide feature introduced in iOS13 for all iOS devices. Dark mode provides a better experience for users, especially when using the iPad in low-light environments. All of your apps and browsers will change to dark mode when this function is turned on.

You can also add this control to the Control Center to quickly change from light to dark mode, or vice versa, within a few seconds.

To change to dark mode manually, head over to Settings>Display & Brightness and click on the "Light" or "Dark" option. You can also toggle the "Automatic" option on if you want to automatically change into dark mode after a set time.

Cut, Copy, and Paste Between iDevices

The advantage of having a well-integrated ecosystem is that you can practically do anything with your devices when connected with the same Apple ID and on the same Wi-Fi network. For example, you can copy a bunch of text on your iPad and send it to your iPhone.

How to achieve tasks like these?

Confirm that both devices are connected with the same Apple ID.

Confirm that both devices are on the same network.

Confirm that Bluetooth is switched on and that both the devices are near each other for a better Bluetooth connection.

Now select a bunch of text on iPad and use your fingers to make a pinch gesture. You will now get the option to "Send to iPhone." Tap on it for the text to be transferred to your iPhone clipboard.

You can also use this technology to send images or any other attachments.

Sharing app links will automatically install the app on your other device after authentication.

Portable Printer

All Apple devices use AirPrint to easily print any files or web pages with the help of a modern printer. AirPrint is integrated with almost every modern printer available now.

Make sure that your iPad and printer are connected to the same Wi-Fi network for the wireless print functionality to work.

On any web page or document, click on the share button icon and tap on the "More Options" button.

You will now be able to see a printer icon and tap on it to head to the next interface.

In this interface, you will have the option to select your printer, how many copies you want to print, and how many pages you want to print if it is a document.

Once the information is entered, click on the "Print" button on the top right corner to complete the job.

Do Not Disturb Mode

Do Not Disturb mode is one of the classic features in the Apple Ecosystem. With this mode on, it becomes easy to ignore calls automatically when you are busy. With iPad

OS15, several new features are added in the name of Focus. Focus helps Apple users customize how they want to use the device in different situations.

To use Do Not Disturb mode, you need to customize Focus settings. To access these settings, head over to Settings>Focus.

Once in the Focus settings, tap on the Do Not Disturb option.

You now need to toggle the Do Not Disturb mode on to activate across your device.

In the settings option, you can add exceptions by adding people and apps that you want to receive notifications from.

At the end of the options list, you can select a time to activate Do Not Disturb mode automatically

Silence Unknown Callers

Spam calls are annoying and are common these days. You can restrict these unknown calls to end automatically with the Focus mode. However, you do not need to turn on "Do Not Disturb" mode to silence these unknown callers every time.

From iPad OS13 onwards, Apple has provided a specific option for users to achieve this task quickly. First, head over to Settings>Phone and toggle the option "Silence Unknown callers" on.

With this turned on, you will not receive any calls from numbers you have never contacted. On the other hand, you will receive calls from numbers you have messaged or communicated with before, even if they are not in your contacts.

Energy-Saving Mode

The iOS low-power mode was popular right from its inception in iPhones from iOS9. iPads, however, have got this feature only on iOS15. The energy-saving mode doesn't just decrease screen brightness or background refresh, it also reduces the overclock processing power of the iPads Central Processing Unit (CPU) to get more usage from the device.

To activate energy-saving mode, head over to Settings>Battery and toggle the low-power mode option on . You can also add it to the Control Center for faster access.

Flash Like a Flashlight

The Camera app usually uses flash to take pictures in low-light backgrounds. The light-emitting diode (LED) flash present in iPads can also act as a flashlight anytime you want to by just clicking on the flashlight icon in your Control Center.

Holding the flashlight button on the Control Center will also provide you with an option to easily increase or reduce the brightness of the flashlight.

Memojis

Memojis are advanced emojis that Apple created for its messaging platform. You can send these emojis to your contacts in the Messages and FaceTime apps. Memojis match your personality and mimic your facial expressions.

To create your own memoji, go to the Messages app and click on the new conversation icon or go to an existing conversation.

Once in the conversation, tap on the memoji button (usually third from the left). You will now be able to see all of the default memojis provided by Apple. There are more than 30 memojis for you to choose from

Click on the "+" button to create your own memoji and to customize different features such as skin tone, hairstyle, eyes, and a lot more.

Once everything is set to your liking, tap on the "Done" button to create the memoji. You can now record voice while sending your memoji to mimic your expressions on your customized avatar.

Chapter 8: Maintenance and battery replacement options

Battery Life Tips

Several things work together to reduce the life of your battery, like plugging the device when on a 100% charge. Below I will list tips that will help to prolong the life of the battery.

It is important not to let your battery get drained totally. It should not go below the 20 percent battery level.

Avoid exposing the device to excessive heat. It is a terrible idea to charge your iPad in a scorching environment.

Quick change from very hot to freezing temperatures is bad for the health of your battery.

Whenever you intend not to use your device for a week and above, ensure to run down the battery to below 80% but not less than 30 percent. Then shut down the iPad entirely.

Do not always fully charge your device when not using it for a long time.

iPad Accessories

The Apple Ecosystem provides different accessories to expand your iPad to a personal computer level quickly. With every new update, iPad OS is becoming efficient enough to support new accessories released by both Apple and third-party companies. Knowing how to easily connect these accessories to your iPad device is essential for device owners.

Apple Keyboard (Magic Keyboard and Smart Folio)

For an iPad to become an alternative to a personal computer, a keyboard and mouse are a must. Fortunately, Apple has constantly focused on improving different keyboard and mouse support for different iPad models. There are also several third-party wireless Bluetooth keyboards and mice which can be connected to your iPad.

Apple provides two different keyboard models for iPad users.

Magic Keyboard for iPad

This is the newest and the most efficient keyboard for an iPad on the market. The Magic Keyboard also comes with an inbuilt trackpad, making it one of the most valuable accessories available in the Ecosystem.

You can connect your iPad magnetically to the case provided with the Magic Keyboard. You can also change your viewing angles easily with the Magic Keyboard, and quickly charge an iPad by charging the keyboard, as Apple has made it possible to charge your iPad by plugging into the keyboard itself.

To connect to the Magic Keyboard, ensure that your Bluetooth is switched on. Head over to Settings>Bluetooth and click on the Magic Keyboard icon to pair it with the device.

To adjust the keyboard brightness during low-light conditions, you can head over to Settings>General>Keyboard>Hardware Keyboard and drag the slider according to your requirements.

Smart Keyboard Folio for iPad

Not all iPad models support Magic Keyboard. For iPad Air and basic iPad models, Apple provides an alternative with the Smart Keyboard Folio. It works just as well as the Magic Keyboard, but comes without a trackpad.

To connect to the Smart Folio Keyboard, ensure that your Bluetooth is switched on. Head over to Settings > Bluetooth and click on the Smart folio keyboard to pair it with the device.

Airpods and Earpods

Airpods have become one of the essential accessories for Apple devices in the past few years. They are typically headphones but with wireless technology. Airpods provide high-quality sound and a flawless microphone that can make calls. They connect to your device using Bluetooth technology.

To connect to Airpods from your device, head over to Settings>Bluetooth and turn on the Bluetooth. Without Bluetooth, it is not possible to connect your Airpods.

Now, head over to the home screen and open your Airpods case for the iPad to detect your Airpods automatically. A graphic pop-up will appear on your home screen. Click on the "Connect" button on this pop-up to automatically pair Airpods to your iPad.

If you don't have Airpods, you can also use earpods that come with a headphone jack or lightning connector to listen to music. All you have to do is insert your earpods connector into the slot to make the iPad use it as output.

Apple Pencil

Apple Pencil is an advanced stylus developed for iPad by Apple. Apple Pencil is fast and accurate and will instantly work with different iPad models. It is essential to know the two types of Apple Pencil models are available for iPad users. The newer iPad models can support the second generation Apple Pencil, whereas the older iPad models (older than 2018) only support the first generation Apple Pencil.

Apple Pencil comes with palm-rejection technology and makes it easy for digital artists to draw on the iPad screen without worrying about any problems that may otherwise be caused by losing tilt control. Apart from professionals, normal users can also use Apple Pencil to take notes, annotate documents, and browse the iPad.

Quick Note Feature

From iPad OS15, you can use the Quick Note feature provided to make notes by swiping up from the bottom right of the screen using an Apple Pencil. The note will be automatically saved to the Notes app. You can draw or scribble with the Quick Note feature.

Apple Mouse and Trackpad

For a complete office setup having a trackpad along with a keyboard is essential. Apple provides excellent trackpads for all iPad models.

To connect to your Magic Trackpad, make sure it is charged and powered on. Head over to Settings, switch on the Bluetooth, and search for new devices to pair it to the device.

Some Gestures for Magic Trackpad:

- To click, press once on the trackpad.

- To hold, press once on the trackpad and hold with one finger.

- To drag and move, click once on the trackpad and hold it while sliding it with your finger.

- Tap once on the Magic Keyboard for it to wake if it is in a locked state.

- With one finger, swipe to the bottom of the screen to go to the home screen from any application.

- To open the control center, swipe with your hand to the top right.

- To open the notification center, swipe with your hand to the top left.

- To switch between apps, swipe either left or right with three fingers.

- To zoom in on any images or maps, use the pinch gesture with your fingers.

While the trackpad provides more gestures for iPad users, you can still use a regular wireless mouse to do a lot of tasks on your iPad.

To connect to a mouse for iPad, head over to Settings>Bluetooth and connect to the mouse. Once connected, you can easily control your iPad using gestures such as click and double-click.

Apart from these official accessories from Apple, you can also connect to third-party accessories such as wireless headphones and controllers using the Bluetooth option available in Settings.

Conclusion

Congratulations on completing this guide. The iPad is one of the most well-known technological advancements in the last ten years. With just a few clicks, you can convert an iPad into a gaming console, workplace tool, or a device for watching videos and listening to music. You may have already noticed the lengthy lines that form outside the Apple store whenever a new iPad is announced. The demand for iPad never goes away. Apple claims to have sold three times as many iPads as they did the year before, particularly during the lockdown.

Now that you've read the book, I would advise seniors to virtually replicate each step on your iPad for effective system operation and in order to help you recall the instructions or specifics given in this book. If you are unsure of the procedures, you can make a straightforward mind map or utilize passive recall strategies like memory palace to remember them exactly as they are.

All relevant areas concerning iPad have been carefully outlined and discussed in detail to make users more familiar with its operations as well as other information not contained elsewhere.

IPads are great devices, and we hope that you will get the most out of your device. If you are a person who gets anxious while dealing with any new technology, then read the simple tricks below to relieve any anxiety that can occur.

New features for translating text and conversations are available in the Translate app, and Swift Playgrounds now lets you create apps for the iPhone and iPad on your iPad. Apple iPad includes capabilities to reduce distractions, a new notification experience, features for FaceTime calls, additional privacy settings, revamped Weather, Maps, and Safari, among other things.

An individual may find it tough to decide which iPad is appropriate for them because there are so many iPads models currently on sale, and a significant amount of money needs to be invested.

No matter how many suggestions you consider, it would be beneficial if you ultimately choose an iPad that meets your needs. Different iPad models serve different purposes and cater to various customer segments. Keep in mind that all these models run the same iPad OS despite having different hardware. Therefore, if you're using a low-end iPad, you should not be concerned about incompatible apps. It's crucial to realize that the Pro models offer some extra software improvements to device owners.

Now that you are more familiar with features and tips on operating your iPad Pro, I am confident that you will enjoy using your device on the new iPad.

Have a great time using your iPad!

Made in the USA
Las Vegas, NV
15 August 2023

76161700R00050